P9-DIA-013

2/11

FER-DE-LANCE

Master Killer!

by Nancy White

Consultant: Raoul Bain, Biodiversity Specialist, Herpetology
Center for Biodiversity and Conservation
American Museum of Natural History
New York, New York

BEARPORT PUBLISHING

New York, New York

Credits

Cover and Title Page, © Gerry Bishop/Visuals Unlimited, Inc.; TOC, © Stephen Dalton/NHPA/Photoshot; 4, © Martin Rogers/Corbis; 5, © Robert Pickett/Papilio/Alamy; 7, © Robert Pickett/Papilio/Alamy; 8, © Joe McDonald/Visuals Unlimited, Inc.; 9, © David South/Alamy; 10, © Michael & Patricia Fogden; 11, © Jany Sauvanet/NHPA/Photoshot; 12, © Michael & Patricia Fogden; 13, © Montford Thierry/Biosphoto/Peter Arnold Inc.; 14L, © Michael & Patricia Fogden; 14R, © Claus Meyer/Minden Pictures; 15, © Rhett Butler/mongabay.com; 16, © Dr. Zoltan Takacs; 17, © Michael Fogden/Animals Animals Enterprises; 18, © David Northcott/DanitaDelimont.com; 19, © Bernard Photo Productions/Animals Animals Enterprises; 20, © Michael & Patricia Fogden; 21, © Michael & Patricia Fogden/Minden Pictures; 22, © Andres Avila Aguilar; 23A, © JH Pete Carmichael/Riser/Getty Images; 23B, © IntraClique/Shutterstock; 23C, © Snowleopard1/Shutterstock; 23D, © Robert Pickett/Papilio/Alamy; 23E, © Dr. Zoltan Takacs; 23F, © Maria Dryfhout/Shutterstock; 23G, © Snowleopard1/Shutterstock; 23H, © Susan Flashman/Shutterstock.

Publisher: Kenn Goin
Senior Editor: Lisa Wiseman
Creative Director: Spencer Brinker
Photo Researcher: Jennifer Bright
Design: Dawn Beard Creative

Library of Congress Cataloging-in-Publication Data

White, Nancy, 1942–
   Fer-de-lance : master killer! / by Nancy White.
      p. cm. — (Fangs)
   Includes bibliographical references and index.
   ISBN-13: 978-1-59716-769-7 (library binding)
   ISBN-10: 1-59716-769-X (library binding)
   1. Fer-de-lance—Juvenile literature. I. Title.

QL666.O69W48 2009
597.96'3—dc22

                    2008041863

For more information, write to Bearport Publishing Company, Inc., 101 Fifth Avenue, Suite 6R, New York, New York 10003. Printed in the United States of America.

10 9 8 7 6 5 4 3 2 1

Contents

Fear in the Forest

As a young man walked through a banana plantation, he didn't notice a huge snake **coiled** on the ground. When he accidentally stepped on it, however, the animal reared up and bit him on the leg. He screamed in pain as two dagger-like **fangs** sank deep into his flesh. He'd been bitten by a fer-de-lance, one of the world's most feared **venomous** snakes. Blood dripped from his wounds and his leg started to swell. Luckily for him, a shot of a special medicine called antivenin (*an*-tee-VEN-uhn) would save his life.

▲ A man working on a banana plantation in Costa Rica

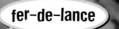

fer-de-lance

There are several types of fer-de-lance snakes. Although scientists have found slight differences among them, they're all very similar.

Hidden Snakes

How can people recognize a fer-de-lance? These snakes come in a range of colors such as dark green, brown, red, pink, or tan. Their backs and sides are marked with dark-colored diamond patterns and crisscrossing yellow bands. Like all snakes, they're covered with **scales**. Some of them are smooth, but the ones on the diamond patterns are velvety.

The snake's colors and patterns camouflage it, or help it blend in with its surroundings. Blending in makes the fer-de-lance hard for enemies and **prey** to see. Even though a fer-de-lance is around six feet (1.83 m) long, its colors help the large snake easily hide under leaves or plants.

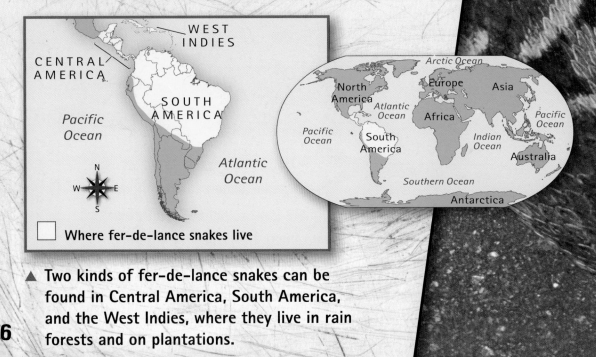

WEST INDIES

CENTRAL AMERICA

SOUTH AMERICA

Pacific Ocean

Atlantic Ocean

N
W   E
S

☐ Where fer-de-lance snakes live

Arctic Ocean

North America

Europe

Asia

Atlantic Ocean

Africa

Pacific Ocean

Pacific Ocean

South America

Indian Ocean

Australia

Southern Ocean

Antarctica

▲ Two kinds of fer-de-lance snakes can be found in Central America, South America, and the West Indies, where they live in rain forests and on plantations.

The name *fer-de-lance* is French. The French word *fer* means "iron." So *fer-de-lance* means "the pointed iron tip on a lance." A lance is a long wooden pole once used as a weapon. The snake was given this name because it has a pointy head.

pointy head

Deadly Habits

Camouflage is one reason the fer-de-lance is dangerous to humans. It can be so hard to spot that a person often disturbs it by accident. That can be a bad mistake because this snake is quick to **strike**.

The fer-de-lance's hunting habits make it dangerous, too. Most snakes avoid places where humans live and work, but this snake will go anywhere to find its favorite food—rats. These animals are often found in fields or buildings on banana and coffee plantations. Many unlucky workers have been bitten after accidentally disturbing a hidden fer-de-lance.

▲ A coiled up fer-de-lance

Fer-de-lance snakes hunt at night. During the day, they stay coiled up under plants or leaves. Unfortunately, that's when people are out working in the fields.

A plantation in Costa Rica

The Killer's Bite

What happens when a fer-de-lance bites? Two long, sharp fangs pierce the **victim**'s flesh. The fangs are hollow, like a doctor's needle. They are connected to sacs on the sides of the snake's head, where venom is made. When the snake bites, this liquid poison shoots out through the fangs and into the victim.

Right after a person is bitten, the painful wound begins to bleed. The snake's venom makes the victim's blood thin and watery. It also breaks down the walls of veins and arteries, which causes bleeding inside the person's body and can lead to death.

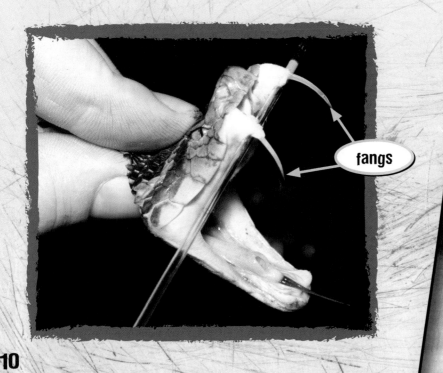

fangs

A nine-year-old girl's foot after being bitten by a fer-de-lance

The fer-de-lance's venom can also destroy a victim's flesh. The area around the bite becomes red and swollen and starts to rot!

Small Prey

While the fer-de-lance can be dangerous to humans, it doesn't hunt or chase them. Like other venomous snakes, it would rather avoid people than attack them.

The reason that the fer-de-lance doesn't hunt humans is that they're too big to eat. All snakes swallow their food whole, and a human can't fit into a fer-de-lance's mouth. This snake usually hunts small animals such as rats, opossums, birds, frogs, lizards, and other snakes. When it does bite a person, the snake is simply defending itself against a possible enemy.

opossum

A fer-de-lance is able to swim and climb trees. Adult snakes, however, spend most of their time on the ground.

Self-Defense

Biting isn't the snake's only defense, however. It often tries to escape an attack or scare enemies away by making a buzzing sound with its tail. The fer-de-lance doesn't have hard rings called rattles on its tail like its relative the rattlesnake. However, it can copy a rattler's sound by moving its tail very quickly among leaves or sticks on the ground.

Hog-nosed skunk ▶

▲ Armadillo

The fer-de-lance's enemies include the armadillo and the hog-nosed skunk. Humans are enemies, too. People often try to kill these snakes because they are afraid of them.

tail

Killer in the Dark

The fer-de-lance does its hunting at night. How does it find its prey in the dark? Like all snakes, it uses its sense of smell. Its forked tongue flicks in and out, bringing the smell of the prey from the air into its mouth.

However, the fer-de-lance depends on something else even more to find its meal—its **pits**. These small round openings, on each side of its face, allow the snake to sense the heat given off by another animal. They tell the snake exactly where the animal is located so that it can strike and kill its prey.

forked tongue

Both the fer-de-lance and the rattlesnake are members of a group of snakes called pit vipers. All these snakes have pits, which they use for detecting prey.

pit

The Killer Strikes

The fer-de-lance doesn't chase its prey. It's known as a "sit-and-wait" hunter. At night, it lies very still on the ground waiting for prey to come near. Then it's mealtime!

When a rat wanders by, the snake senses the animal's exact position with its pits. The killer then rears off the ground and forms a curved shape, like the letter S, with its upper body. In a flash, the snake strikes, sinking its fangs into the rat's flesh. Once the deadly venom is injected, the snake lets go. The rat tries to escape but doesn't get far. The venom soon kills it.

▲ A fer-de-lance getting ready to attack

A fer-de-lance feeding on a rodent

A fer-de-lance easily finds the rat it has poisoned with its venom by using its pits. Once found, the dead rat is swallowed whole.

Born Alive!

Unlike most other snakes, fer-de-lance babies do not hatch from eggs. They are born alive—sometimes 80 at the same time! While less than half the size of adults, they can still hunt and kill. They attack small prey such as frogs, lizards, and other snakes.

The little snakes differ from adults in many ways, however. The colors of the young are brighter, and their tails are lighter. Also, they spend more time in trees than on the ground. Yet a newborn fer-de-lance has the same deadly venom as its parents. Even the baby is a master killer!

▲ **A young fer-de-lance biting a frog**

Fer-de-lance babies use their light-colored tails to get food. A frog, for example, might think the tail is something good to eat, like a worm or a caterpillar. When the prey comes close the baby snake snaps it up!

a young fer-de-lance

frog

Fang Facts

- Every year hundreds of people are bitten by fer-de-lance snakes. This master killer causes more human deaths each year than any other snake in North America and South America.

- Like other pit vipers, the fer-de-lance has fangs that fold up against the roof of its mouth when they're not being used. Then when the snake strikes, the fangs unfold and spring forward to bite the victim.

- The fangs of the fer-de-lance are up to one inch (2.5 cm) long. Only one other snake in North America and South America—the bushmaster—has longer fangs for a snake the same size.

- While the venom of the fer-de-lance is deadly, some scientists think it could be used to make medicines to save people's lives. One scientist, for example, is working on a medicine to help people who have heart disease.

fangs

Glossary

coiled
(KOILD) wound around and around in loops

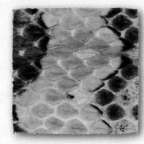

scales
(SKAYLZ) small pieces of hard skin that cover the body of a snake

fangs
(FANGZ) long pointy teeth

strike
(STRIKE) to hit or attack something

pits
(PITS) body parts on a pit viper's face that are able to sense heat

venomous
(VEN-uhm-uhss) full of poison

prey
(PRAY) animals that are hunted and eaten by other animals

victim
(VIK-tuhm) an animal that is attacked or killed by another animal

Index

Read More

Fiedler, Julie. *Vipers.* New York: PowerKids Press (2008).

Klein, Adam G. *Pit Vipers.* Edina, MN: ABDO Publishing (2006).

Singer, Marilyn. *Venom.* Plain City, OH: Darby Creek Publishing (2007).

Learn More Online

To learn more about the fer-de-lance, visit
www.bearportpublishing.com/Fangs

About the Author

Nancy White has written many science and nature books
for children. She lives in the Hudson River Valley,
in a small village just north of New York City.